Thomas John Bailey

# English Orders and Papal Supremacy

A Brief Manual of Historical Facts

Thomas John Bailey

**English Orders and Papal Supremacy**
*A Brief Manual of Historical Facts*

ISBN/EAN: 9783744641258

Printed in Europe, USA, Canada, Australia, Japan

Cover: Foto ©ninafisch / pixelio.de

More available books at **www.hansebooks.com**

# ENGLISH ORDERS

AND

# PAPAL SUPREMACY:

## A Brief Manual of Historical Facts.

BY THE

## REV. T. J. BAILEY, B.A.,

CORPUS CHRISTI COLLEGE, CAMBRIDGE.

LONDON AND OXFORD:

JAMES PARKER & CO., 377 STRAND.

Brighton: G. Wakeling, North Street.

1868.

# PREFACE.

THE compiler of the following Manual wishes
to state distinctly that no pretensions to ori-
ginality are here put forth by him; the
Manual is simply a compilation from various
authors who have written on the two subjects,
such as Courayer, Chancellor Harrington,
Barrow, Neander, Dr Prideaux, Ffoulkes,
Allies, Spanheim's Ecclesiastical Annals, the
Bishops of Ely and Brechin, Dr Pusey, Dr
Oldknow, Rev. J. C. Chambers, &c. &c., and
is intended simply as a help to those who
have neither the time nor the opportunity
of consulting larger volumes.

*Holy Week*, 1868.

# ENGLISH ORDERS

## AND

# PAPAL SUPREMACY.

---

### THE VALIDITY OF ENGLISH ORDERS.

THE compilation of the following Manual has
arisen from a desire to supply a want which
has often been felt by the compiler, in common with
many of his brother priests in the Church of England, in replying to an oft-repeated question, " Can
you give me any short decisive arguments in reply
to the charge of the Church of Rome, that our communion is not a true branch of Christ's Holy Catholic Church ?  Two points, viz., " The Validity of
our Orders," and " The claim of the Pope to Universal Supremacy," at once suggested themselves on
which it would be possible, by a reference to
authentic records, — themselves incontrovertible,
except upon a general charge of forgery, which

A

charge, by its sweeping condemnation, cuts the ground from under its own feet,—to state *facts*, not *mere* opinions, in reply to this question.

With regard to the first we at once admit, that upon the ordination of Archbishop Parker all the others after him depend, and that the validity of this carries with it the clear succession of the Episcopate in England.

To the validity of his ordination three objections are raised :—

1st, As to the fact of his consecration itself.

2d, That there is no proof of the consecration of Barlow, the first of the four consecrators of Parker.

3d, That the form of the consecration itself rendered it invalid.

Now it is an historical fact that Cardinal Pole, the successor of Cranmer, surviving Queen Mary but a few hours, Elizabeth on coming to the Crown found the Archbishopric of Canterbury at her disposal, and that she at once selected Matthew Parker to fill that see. She therefore addressed, on the 18th of July 1559, a *congé d'élire* to the Chapter of Canterbury. Accordingly, on the 1st day of August, the Chapter did choose him for their Archbishop, and certified this election to the Queen, in order that she might give it effect by her letters patent. (See Rymer's Records.) She did so, and on the 9th of September directed a Commission to Cuthbert, Bishop of Durham, Gilbert, Bishop of Bath, David, Bishop of Peterborough, Anthony,

Bishop of Llandaff, William Barlow, bishop, and John Scory, also bishop, for the consecration and confirmation of Parker.

This Commission was never executed—the three first named bishops refusing to take part, (as they shortly afterwards also refused to take the Oath of Supremacy, and were deposed in consequence), consequently, the Queen, on the 6th of December, caused another Commission to be directed to Anthony, Bishop of Llandaff, William Barlow, formerly Bishop of Bath, now Bishop-elect of Chichester, John Scory, formerly Bishop of Chichester, now Bishop-elect of Hereford, Miles Coverdale, formerly Bishop of Exeter, Richard (for John) of Bedford, and John of Thetford, suffragan Bishops, and John Bale, Bishop of Ossory, to the end that all, or at least four of them, should proceed to the consecration of Parker.

Of these the Bishop of Llandaff, although he had taken the Oath of Supremacy, did not take part in the consecration, on account either of his infirmities, or for some other reason not known; so that Barlow found himself at the head of the Commission, and assisted by John Scory, Bishop-elect of Hereford, Miles Coverdale, late Bishop of Exeter, and John Hodgskins, suffragan of Bedford, confirmed Parker's election on the 9th of December, the actual consecration being performed at Lambeth, on Sunday, the 17th of December 1559, by the same bishops who had confirmed the election.

The instrument recording this fact is to be found in Archbishop Bramhall's works, p. 1051; Burnet, vol. i., Appendix; Courayer, Appendix. Mason and Collier have given either large extracts, or the substance of the whole; and the original records themselves are still to be seen in the registers of Canterbury, and in the valuable manuscript library of Corpus Christi College, Cambridge, of which college the Archbishop was himself a member, and for some time master.

To these may be added the mandate of Barlow for the enthroning of Parker, bearing date the 31st of December; that of the Archdeacon of Canterbury to the Chapter for the same purpose, dated 1st of January 1560; the Procuration of Parker, addressed to Edward Searles and some others of his chaplains, to take possession in his name, dated the 2d of January; and the Act of Investiture, the 21st of March.

Now as every one of the documents above mentioned are open to examination, it is very clear that the forgery, if one there be, must be of an extent before unparalleled, seeing that it involves the falsification of records of the most solemn nature, including those of the Chancery, the Signet Office, the Exchequer, the Registries, the Bishop, the Dean and Chapter, besides the counterfeiting the hands and seal of the Sovereign, the Lord Chancellor, the Lord Privy Seal, the clerks, and the public notaries. And here we may add, and this is a point of the utmost importance, "that the four notaries who

attested Cardinal Pole's consecration (about which
no doubt whatever has been at any time alleged)
signed also the Act of Consecration of Parker; the
comparison of their handwriting affording a decisive
proof of the authenticity of the act," (Dr Elrington's
Validity of English Ordination.) One further argument related by Godwin would seem to put the
matter out of dispute as to the truth or falsehood of
the registers of Canterbury, and, by a natural in-
ference, of all the others—viz., that permission was
given by George Abbot, Archbishop of Canterbury,
to four (Roman) Catholics, three of whom were
Jesuits, to examine the register as much as they
pleased, in the presence of the Bishops of London,
Durham, Ely, Bath, Lincoln, and Rochester. They
did so, and promised to testify to the truth of what
they had seen. It is quite true to add also, that
upon their making a second application for permission to take the book away with them, that they
might examine it with greater attention, they were
refused, and told that those books were not allowed
to be removed; that they might examine them again
upon the place, but they could not be trusted in their
hands. This refusal is insisted upon to give a colour
to the charge of forgery. To this adds Courayer:
" But, in truth, was this a reasonable request? and
ought they not to have expected such an answer?
If this were sufficient to create a suspicion that the
registers were forged, what record can be free from
suspicion?—nothing being so unusual as to entrust

to strangers or to enemies essential documents, whose preservation is of immeasurable importance?"

A further testimony to the genuineness of the documents is added by Courayer, who states that, upon an application made by himself, permission was at once freely granted to him, in the presence of four witnesses, two of whom were (Roman) Catholics, to assure himself more strongly of the authenticity of these records, and a certificate signed by them, the original of which is now in the library of Paris, testified that the record printed in Archbishop Bramhall's book is entirely conformable to the registers.

To these facts it is alleged that this record and these registers to which I have referred, have been produced only by those who are interested in falsifying them, and who, being sole guardians of these monuments, could with impunity forge, or at least alter them. To this I reply, it is at all times an easy matter to raise a suspicion; the difficulty lies in the possibility of substantiating it. In the present case it is impossible to lay the charge of forgery or corruption upon the record of Parker's consecration in the registers wherein it is recorded, without throwing the same suspicion on the public records collected by Rymer; for between all these the harmony is so perfect as at once to negative this charge, and a second reason, which ought to be more convincing, is, "that if they had wished to forge records, they would not have confined themselves to these, and they would have dressed them up otherwise than they are. For instance, they would have given us the record of Barlow's consecration, which is so essential in this affair; they would have omitted the clause in the mandate for Parker's consecration, from which so much advantage is endeavoured to be taken against him. In a word, they would have omitted nothing essential, nor inserted anything that was to their prejudice. Besides, too, if they were to forge a relation, why should they not make the consecration to have been performed according to the rites of the Roman Pontifical, rather than according to King Edward's ordinal. It would have cost them no more forgery, and they would thereby have prejudiced the (Roman) Catholics in favour of their ordination, which it was their interest to do. This, nevertheless, was not done. The forgery is therefore a mere chimera, and has no other foundation than an unreasonable distrust and prejudice." These are the words of Courayer, himself a (Roman) Catholic, having been canon regular and librarian of S. Geneviéve, at Paris.

The limits of a small manual like the present forbid the production of further evidence on this point; but this much I feel it right to add, that the more the question is examined into, the more conclusive will it appear, so large and weighty a mass of independent evidence being at hand, as to preclude the possibility of collusion or falsehood.

The following remarks by the able editor of Bramhall's Works in the Library of Anglo-Catholic
Theology, (the Rev. A. W. Haddan, Fellow and
Tutor of Trinity College, Oxford,) seem so particularly to the purpose, that although somewhat a
repetition of what has been already said, yet I feel
it right to subjoin them :—

"As the case stands, I may be permitted to say,
that the result of a tolerably minute examination of
the evidence upon the subject is this : that if any one
is disposed to question the truth of the account given
in the Lambeth Register, he must be prepared to
assert the forgery, not only of the Register itself,—
and the first volume of Archbishop Parker's Register,
which is the volume in question, consists of 411
pages, containing a mass of circumstantial entries
upon a great variety of subjects,—but of the Registers also of the several sees and chapters throughout the kingdom, for the period referred to, (so
far as they are preserved, or as it has been found
possible to consult them ;) of many pages of entries
in the Registers of the Prerogative Court of Canterbury ; of thirty or forty documents in the Rolls ; of
a mass of contemporary letters and other documents
preserved in the Library of Corpus Christi College,
Cambridge, with the existence of which Mason, an
Oxonian, (who is the person accused, most absurdly,
of forging the Register in 1613,) was unacquainted ;
of other, also contemporary documents, preserved
in the State Paper Office, likewise unknown to

Mason; of others, (which are by themselves enough
to prove the case,) preserved at Zurich, and unknown in England until 1685, seventy-two years
after Mason's book was published; of Archbishop
Parker's book, " De Antiquitate Britanniæ Ecclesiæ,"
as privately printed by him in 1572, a work of
which twenty-two copies were known to exist (out
of fifty originally printed) in 1724; of a Puritan
translation of a life of Parker, (the original of which
is in Corpus Christi College Library, Cambridge,)
containing a table of the consecrations in question,
according mainly with the Register, and printed in
1574, of which several copies exist; of pp. 1490,
1491, in the middle of vol. iii. of Holinshed's
Chronicle, as first published in 1586; and lastly, of
at least three other printed authorities prior to 1613,
all of which evidences are independent of each
other, bear no signs whatever of want of genuineness, and tally to a very minute degree of accuracy;
and he must be prepared to do this upon the
testimony of two, or at the most three, obscure con-
troversialists, the earliest fifty-four years after the
event, writing in foreign countries, and avowedly
upon mere hearsay, whose evidence is in itself
rendered absolutely unworthy of credit, by the un-
disguised virulence and palpable ignorance of the
writings in which it is found. Such is in brief
the balance of testimony upon which he must be
prepared to surrender a consistent, probable, and
rational narrative, and to adopt in its stead a

supposition at once incongruous, improbable, and absurd."

Hitherto I have made no allusion to the so-called Nag's-Head Story. One reason of my not having done so is that its falsehood is so apparent that few, if any, persons of understanding are found to receive it at the present day; yet, as its omission might suggest a doubt of an entire disbelief in it, I briefly add a few remarks upon it.

The fable, for such it is, as given by (Roman) Catholic writers,—viz., Sanders, Le Quien, Constable, Sacrobosco, Fitz-Simon, Wadsworth, Killison, &c., is briefly as follows :—In the beginning of Queen Elizabeth's reign, the vacant sees being about to be filled up, those who were nominated and elected met by appointment in London, at an inn known by the name of the Nag's-Head, in Cheapside. There they were to be met and consecrated by the Bishop of Llandaff, but Bonner, Bishop of London, having received an intimation of what was about to be done, threatened the Bishop of Llandaff with excommunication if he consecrated them, and he accordingly refused to do so; that they then addressed themselves to Scory, (whom they call an apostate monk, although his consecration as Bishop, in the reign of Edward VI., can be clearly proved,) and that he laid the Bible upon the head of each of them, as they knelt before him, saying, "Take thou authority to preach the Word of God sincerely;" and so they rose up all Bishops.

In reply to this, to say nothing of the important facts, that no man is allowed by law to consecrate or to be consecrated but in a sacred place, with due matter and form, and this by four bishops, or three at the least, and after the election of the Dean and Chapter has been duly confirmed, and upon the mandate or commission of the Sovereign under the Great Seal of England, under the pain of a præmunire, we have this miserable story, resting upon no worthier testimony than an unknown person named Thomas Neal, then an officer of Bishop Bonner's household, so that to cite authorities to refute does seem, as it were, to give it an importance which of itself it could never possess; nevertheless, for the reason previously stated, I add briefly a few remarks. First, against the statement of Neal we have that of Lord Charles Howard, Earl of Nottingham, at one time Lord High Admiral of England, who, in the year 1616, being asked by a friend, "Whether or no he was invited to honour the consecration of Archbishop Parker and the solemnity thereof with his presence?" answered, "That he was indeed invited, and earnestly entreated to be present at it." Being again asked, "To what place he was invited?" and particularly whether it was to the Nag's-Head? his lordship replied, "By no means, but to the palace at Lambeth;" whither he also declared he went on the day appointed for that very purpose. He, moreover, positively averred that he was also present, with many other noble

lords, at the entertainment on the very same day of
the consecration; and if this itself were not sufficient, we have the public attestation to the falsehood
of the story, of the Bishop of Durham, July 17, 1658.
Further, there is this very significant fact, that the
story itself was not heard of for fifty years after it
was alleged to have occurred, and is not to be met
with in any authors who have written in Parker's
own time, and lastly, the story affirms that all the
bishops nominated to the vacant sees were then consecrated with Parker, but all the records, both civil
and ecclesiastical, testify the contrary; for, taking
the date of Archbishop Parker's letters patent, on
the 6th day of December 1559, we find commissions
issued to him for the consecration of Grindall,
Cox, and Sands, who were consecrated together,
December 21st, 1559; then for Bullingham, Lovel,
and Davies, who were consecrated January 21st,
1560; then for Bentham and Barclay, who were
consecrated March 24th, 1560; and in the year following for Horn, consecrated February 16th, 1560;
Alley, consecrated July 14th, 1560; Scandler, consecrated February 11th, 1560; and Pilkington,
consecrated March 2d, 1560. Copies of these commissions are to be seen recorded verbatim both in
the rolls of the Archbishop's Register and in the
rolls of the Chancery. To this I add the remark of
Dr Lingard, who, while fully denouncing the story
as false, says it probably arose from the fact that the
commissioners, having confirmed the election, (at

Bow Church,) dined together at the Nag's-Head, the inn chiefly frequented by the clergy at that period, being also very near to the church; but it is also a known fact that Dr Parker was confirmed by proxy, and was not personally present at Bow Church, or at the dinner afterwards – his proxies, whom he named on the 7th of December, being Dr Nicolas Bullingham, and William May, Dean of St Paul's.

The second objection to the Validity of English Orders rests upon a pretence that Barlow, chief consecrator of Parker, was himself not consecrated, and therefore unable to consecrate another, and the foundation for this pretence is, "that Archbishop Cranmer's Register, which contains the ordinations performed by himself, or by his order, does not contain that of Barlow, so that the record of it could never be found." Next, that in Rymer's Collection of Records, there is a Commission of Queen Elizabeth's, addressed to Parker, already consecrated Archbishop of Canterbury, to confirm and *consecrate* Barlow Bishop of Chichester; accordingly it is said, if he had been consecrated when he ordained (*i.e.*, consecrated) Parker, would Parker have received a commission to consecrate him himself; and lastly, that Bonner, Bishop of London, when he threatened Anthony, Bishop of Llandaff, with excommunication if he meddled in the ordination of Parker, would not have failed to make the same threat to Barlow if he had thought him a bishop;

and that his not having done so was a clear proof that he did not believe him to be such, as he could not have been ignorant of it had it been true. These objections I now proceed to take in order, applying to them the same test as before—viz., the appeal to documents of whose authenticity there is no doubt whatever.   First, then, we have historic evidence.   Wharton, the author of the " Anglica Sacra," says,—" William Barlow, at that time Prior of the Canons Regular of Bisham, of the order of S. Augustine, having been elected Bishop by the Dean and Chapter of S. Asaph, in the year 1536, January the 16th, was confirmed on the 23d of February following, by Thomas, Archbishop of Canterbury."

Next, Le Neve, the author of the " Fasti Ecclesiæ Anglicanæ," says,—" William Barlow, S.T.P., was elected Jan. 16, 1535, confirmed Feb. 23 following."   Certainly both of these speak only of his confirmation, but his consecration must have followed soon after, both because the laws of Henry VIII. required the ceremony of consecration to be performed within twenty days after confirmation, on pain of incurring the penalties of a præmunire, and also because in the parliament summoned on the 27th of April there is mention made of his presence as bishop, together with his presence also in the Convocation assembled at the same time. And here let me add that the fact of his being summoned as Bishop of S. David's is explained by his translation to that see in the month of April. Mr Strype also, the author of the "Life of Cranmer," without any hesitation places Barlow's consecration in the year 1535.

The silence then of Cranmer's Register is no decisive proof of the omission of this consecration. For, as it has been very well observed by Francis Mason, in his "Defence of the Ministry of the Church of England," there are many others who have also been omitted, whose consecrations are notwithstanding very certain. For instance, neither Gardiner's nor that of Fox is to be found. Again, Bishop King, suffragan of Lincoln, was consecrated in 1541, yet neither is his to be found. To these may be added the names of Sampson of Chichester, Bell of Worcester, Day of Chichester, Latimer of Worcester, and several others, whose confirmations and consecrations are not to be found in the Arch-Episcopal Registers; and even of Cardinal Pole, who was recognised as Canonical Primate of all England by the Pope and the Bishops of England, there is no proof that he was ever validly consecrated, for not one of his seven consecrators can be proved, according to the Roman theory, to have been canonical bishops. The silence then of the register is clearly no convincing proof. But there is an important link in the argument for his consecration which must not be overlooked. It is a well-known fact, that although before the time of Edward III. there are some examples of bishops sitting in

Parliament before their consecration, there is not one example to be met with since that time. Full explanations of the usage on this point are given both by Archbishop Bramhall and Bishop Burnet. According to the latter, the rule is, that to have a seat in the House of Lords, it is necessary to present the king's warrant, by virtue of which one was put into possession of the temporalities, and this instrument is never given but upon the certificate of consecration.

Now, in Rymer's Collection, (vol. xiv. pp. 563 and 737,) we have two writs for calling parliaments, one in 1536, the other in 1541. In both of these the Bishop of S. David's, who then was Barlow, is summoned like the rest, and Mason adds, that in the parliament of 1539, Barlow, then Bishop of S. David's, made his appearance in person twenty-seven times in the first session, and fifteen times in the second, consequently he must have been consecrated before. Moreover, his name appears in the Convocation summoned at the same time, and under Henry VIII., in whose time the ecclesiastical rules were observed with sufficient exactness, he never would have taken his place, nor have signed articles therein drawn up, his name, moreover, appearing before that of another bishop, if he had not been consecrated.

Further evidence is given of his presence at the several Synods of 1537, 1540, and 1552. But a stronger proof than any remains; there is a record in Cranmer's Register of the Consecration of Arthur Bulkeley, Bishop of Bangor, A.D. 1541, in which Barlow's name stands before that of the Bishop of Gloucester; may we not ask, would a bishop not consecrated have been suffered in those times to officiate at such a solemnity ?

It is further proved by Parker's Register, that at the first ordination performed by that prelate, Dec. 21, 1559, Barlow was one of the consecrators; and yet one proof further we may add, drawn from an instrument which is found in the Canterbury Registers. In the commission drawn up by the Chapter of Canterbury for the government of the Church of Bath, during the vacancy of that see, it is said to be vacant " by the free and voluntary resignation of W. Barlow, the last bishop and pastor of that church; and this same clause is found in the *congé d'élire* directed to the Chapter of Bath by Queen Mary, dated March 13, 1554.

The second objection arising from the presence of the word "consecrate," in the commission issued by Queen Elizabeth to Parker in 1559, to install Barlow in the see of Chichester, has at first sight some degree of plausibility; as from this it is concluded that, if he had been consecrated in 1536, the Queen would not have given a commission to Parker to consecrate him in 1559. In answer to this, it may be said that there are several mandates in existence, addressed to metropolitans, to confirm the translation of bishops already consecrated, and

B

to install them, in which the term "consecrate" is found; and, on the other hand, in other mandates, drawn up for the confirmation and consecration of new bishops, the term "consecrate" is omitted where it is really wanted, so that this objection possesses no real foundation; but the truth is, as a reference to the original will show, both in Parker's Register and the archives of the Tower, the term consecrate is not to be found at all, but is an unfortunate mistake of Rymer in transcribing. To this I may add the words of Camden, an almost contemporary writer, who says, speaking of Archbishop Parker: "He afterwards consecrated Edmund Grindal. . . . . He also confirmed William Barlow, who in the reign of Henry VIII. had been Bishop of S. David's, and afterwards of Bath, in the Bishopric of Chichester." Here, too, it may be fitting to add, that although Barlow was consecrated Bishop of S. Asaph, he was never installed in that see, but translated to S. David's before his installation—a fact the more worth recording by reason of its rarity. A parallel instance might be quoted of William Juxon, who, in the year 1633, had been chosen Bishop of Hereford; but before he was consecrated and installed, he was translated to London, in which see he was confirmed October 23, 1633, and consecrated on the 27th of the same month.

The third and last objection—viz., that when Bonner threatened Anthony, Bishop of Llandaff, with excommunication, if he took part in the ordination of Parker, he would not have failed to send the same menace to Barlow if he had believed him to be a bishop. But as I have already shown above that the whole story of the Nag's-Head is an absurd fable, the story of the threats of Bonner falls to the ground likewise, as they never were issued at all; and besides, even if he had desired to do so, Bonner had not the power to threaten excommunication, for he was himself looked upon as deposed, so that he had, in fact, no jurisdiction over the person whom he is supposed to have menaced. And further, at the most, he would only have had the right to prevent the performance of such an office against his will in a church within his own jurisdiction; and, as the author of the "Antiquities of the British Church" observes, who gives a list of them, there are many churches in London belonging immediately to the Metropolitan—the Church of S. Mary le Bow, in which Parker was confirmed, being one of them; to which I may add the Palace of Lambeth, in the chapel of which Parker was consecrated.

It remains now to consider briefly the third and last point touching the validity of Parker's consecration—viz., "that the form of the consecration itself rendered it invalid."

This objection being raised through the addition of certain words in the ordinal of Edward VI. which do not occur in the Roman, and the objection being further supposed to be strengthened by the alteration made in our own ordinal in 1662,—as if that were a tacit consent on our side that before this alteration was made our ordinal was not sufficient, and therefore no orders could be conferred thereby, —it would seem to be a sufficient answer to this to refer to the practice of the primitive Church with respect to the matter and form of ordination, and then to compare the respective ordinals of Rome and England, and note their difference and agreement. Here, too, it will scarcely be out of place to quote a remark of the learned Camden, which, although it may be objected to, as being only given by him as a *report*, yet is singularly confirmed by Lord Chief-Justice Coke, in a charge at the assizes held by him at Norwich, August 4, 1606, three years only after Queen Elizabeth's death :—

"It is reported," says Camden, "that the Pope, Pius IV., promised (through the Abbe Vincent Parpaglia, his secret envoy to Elizabeth) that he would confirm the English Liturgy by his authority . . . . provided she would join herself to the Church of Rome, and acknowledge the primacy of the Roman See." And the words of the Lord Chief-Justice confirming this are: "The Pope wrote a letter to Elizabeth, in which he consented to approve the Book of Common Prayer as used among us, and that he would authorise us to use it, if her Majesty would receive it from him, and upon his authority; and this is the truth touching Pope Pius IV., which I have often heard from the Queen's own mouth. And I have frequently conferred with noblemen of the highest rank in the State who had seen and read the Pope's letter on this subject, as I have related it to you."

This of itself would be an answer to the objection; as, if either the matter or form of King Edward's ordinal had been insufficient, it would not be likely for a moment that the Pope, who would of course be fully aware of the invalidity, if such existed, would give his sanction to the book itself. But we need not rest upon this as our reply to the objection.

First, then, as to the practice of the apostles in the primitive Church, the slightest reference to Holy Scripture is sufficient to prove here, that the ordaining both of bishops and priests was by imposition of hands, and prayer, and fasting; and a reference to the learned work of Morinus would furnish us with abundant proofs that such continued to be the practice of the Church, and that the addition of other ceremonies, however fitting to the dignity of the rite, were yet not essential to its validity. To this may be added a further confirmation, by a reference to the Greek and oriental ordinations, which unanimously agree on this point; and these ordinations the Roman Church has ever held valid, and a great authority in that Church, S. Alphonsus Liguori, affirms that imposition of hands is alone the essentially necessary matter, and the words "Receive the Holy Ghost," the necessary *form.*

And in support of this, he gives the names of many learned theologians, and establishes it also by the Council of Trent; first, by a reference to the chapter on Extreme Unction, which says that its proper ministers are "either bishops, or priests rightly ordained by them, with the imposition of the hands of the priesthood." Here is given the *matter* essential for orders; again, in chapter iii., *de ordine*, after having affirmed that "grace is conferred by ordination, which is performed by words and external signs," it continues "for the apostle saith, I admonish thee that thou stir up the grace of God which is in thee by the imposition of my hands," showing again that the grace is given by imposition of hands as the matter. The third passage is in canon iv., *de sacrā ordine*, where it says, "If any one shall say that the Holy Spirit is not given through sacred ordination, and that therefore bishops in vain say, 'Receive the Holy Ghost,' or that a character is not impressed by it, let him be anathema." Here the words "Receive the Holy Ghost, are given as the *form* of orders." S. Alphonsus farther argues, that besides the imposition of hands, nothing else is of essential necessity, "because the Greeks are ordained by the sole imposition of hands; and if the ordination of Greeks by the sole imposition of hands is valid, so must all the ordination of Latins be valid." Bishop Burnet writes as follows :—" Scripture mentions only the imposition of hands and prayer.

In the apostolical constitutions in the fourth Council of Carthage, there was no more used." Afterwards he adds, (speaking of course of his own time,) "Morinus, a learned priest of the Oratorian order, has published the most ancient rituals, by which it appears how these offices swelled in every age by some new addition."

About the middle of the sixth century, they anointed and blessed the priest's hands in some parts of France, though the Irish Church never used anointing, nor was it in the Roman Church two ages after that; for Pope Nicolaus I. (860) plainly says it was never used in the Church of Rome. In the eighth century the priest's vestments were given with a special benediction, while not till the tenth century was there any delivery of the chalice and paten.

Collier, quoting from the same Morinus, speaks to the same effect, summing up his argument, "that prayer and imposition of hands are the only essentials in ordination."

Assuming, which we have the fullest right to do, that prayer and imposition of hands are the only essentials to ordination, it is further objected that though the "matter" of Parker's ordination may be admitted, yet was the "form" unknown to the whole Church, and one of which no trace is to be found in all the pontificals of the Christian world. To meet this, we must first examine exactly wherein the essence of this form consists, whether in a certain formula of words as this, " Receive the Holy Ghost," or in certain prayers, fixed and uniform in all churches, or in prayers in general, such as every church thinks fit to make choice of, and use together with imposition of hands.

To the first, Morinus says these words appear in *none* of the *ancient* Latin Rituals, even in many modern ones no mention is made of them. Another writer, Martene, confirms this opinion, "that they were unknown to all antiquity, so much so that they are scarcely found in any pontifical that is four hundred years old." Besides this, it is well known that neither the Greeks nor Syrians use them. To the second we reply, that the mere inspection of the ancient pontificals, or of the rituals of the different churches, shows that the prayers used, though agreeing in substance, were different either in the choice or arrangement of the words, or in the words themselves.

It remains, therefore, that the invocation of the Holy Ghost in general, upon the Bishop-elect, it is that makes the " form," and the imposition of hands " the matter" of the ordination. Was there, then, any omission or defect in Parker's ordination on these points? Turning to the record of it, we find these decisive words : "After certain prayers and suffrages to God, according to the form prescribed in the book established by the authority of Parliament, the Bishops of Chichester and Hereford, the suffragan Bishop of Bedford, and Miles Coverdale, laying their hands upon the Archbishop, say in English, 'Take the Holy Ghost,' &c." Clearly, then, we have here *loth* the essentials, and therefore the objection can only refer to the alteration in the ordinal of Edward VI., and with regard to this, we shall have no difficulty in coming to a conclusion that here, at least, no one but a most determined opponent could possibly have found fault, and that there is nothing more false than to say that, because the form of prayer in the English ordinal differs from the Roman, yet contains the same substance, it is therefore invalid. The essence of the prayer, as I have observed already, consists in the invocation of the Holy Ghost, to obtain for the Bishop-elect all the graces of which he has need for the due discharge of his ministry. One example will, perhaps, be sufficient to show this, although more could be easily given: —After the hymn "Veni Creator" has been sung, in the prayer following occur these words, " Grant, we beseech Thee, to this Thy servant such grace that he may ever-more be ready to spread abroad Thy gospel, and glad tidings of reconcilement to God, and to use the authority given unto him, not to destroy, but to save; not to hurt, but to help," &c.: which words clearly correspond to those of the pontifical, where we read :—" Da ei Domine claves regni cælorum, ut utatur, non glorietur, potestate quam tribuis in ædificationem, non in destructionem." (Give him, O Lord, the keys of the kingdom of heaven, that he may make use of, not glory in, the power which Thou givest for edification, not for destruction.)

So far then, continues Courayer, whose learned argument I have been making use of, it will be difficult to point out any defect of the ordination prescribed by King Edward's formulary. But there is more if, as some persons contend, the form of ordination be contained in the words, " Receive the Holy Ghost," (although, as I have above shown, this view is untenable, the words not being found in the ancient pontificals, or used by the Greeks.) Here we have the most perfect concord, for at the imposition of hands in the Roman form is said by the consecrator, " Receive the Holy Ghost ;" so in the English ordinal we find the same words, " Take the Holy Ghost," the sense and meaning of which is certainly neither altered nor destroyed by the addition in King Edward's book of the remainder of the sentence, " and remember that thou stir up the grace of God which is in thee by the imposition of our hands ; for God has not given us the spirit of fear, but of power and soberness." So far then we might consider the validity of the consecration, both as to matter and form, beyond a doubt, but that there is one more objection raised, which, if we were to leave unnoticed, might suggest the idea that it was not possible to meet it ; but the truth is, the objection falls to the ground by its own inherent weakness ; for it is stated that the form made use of in the English ordinal appeared so defective to the bishops who had the care of revising the ritual in king Charles II.'s time, 1662, as leaving it equivocal whether it was being used for a priest or bishop, they therefore added some further words to the formula, "Receive the Holy Ghost"—for the priests, "for the office and work of a priest in the Church of God, now committed unto thee by the imposition of our hands;" and for the bishops, "for the office and work of a bishop in the Church of God, now committed unto thee by the imposition of our hands."

This objection is false, both in fact and in intention; in fact, because, besides that the prayers for the two ordinations are different, the very formulæ in question are not alike, for that for the ordination of bishops runs in these words: "Take the Holy Ghost, and remember that thou stir up the grace of God which is in thee by imposition of hands; for God hath not given us the spirit of fear, but of power, and love, and soberness;" while that for priests is as follows: "Receive the Holy Ghost; whose sins thou dost forgive, they are forgiven; and whose sins thou dost retain, they are retained. And be thou a faithful dispenser of the word of God, and of His holy sacraments; in the name of the Father, and of the Son, and of the Holy Ghost. Amen."

It is false also in intention, for a reference to history proves, as Dean Prideaux has already shown, "that the alterations, or rather explanatory additions made in the ordinal in the year 1662, were not inserted out of any respect to the controversy we have with the Church of Rome, but only to silence a cavil of the Presbyterians, who from the old ordinal drew an argument to prove that there was no difference between a bishop and a priest, because (as they say) their offices were not at all distinguished in the words whereby they were conferred on them when ordained, or any new power given a bishop which he had not before as a priest."

There is, too, a very important fact, which, as Dr Pusey remarks, who quotes it in his " Eirenicon," has indeed escaped observation, " that the form adopted at the consecration of Archbishop Parker was carefully framed on the old form used at the consecration of Archbishop Chichele a century before." The use of the form was exceptional, having been resorted to at a time when the English Church did not acknowledge either of the claimants of the Papacy.

The tradition of that consecration was then only a century old. It was of the providence of God that they had that precedent to fall back upon. But the selection of this one precedent (amidst the number of archbishops consecrated in obedience to Papal bulls, in which case the form was wholly different) shows how careful Parker and his consecrators were to follow the ancient precedents."

It remains now only to add, in conclusion, the testimony of eminent Romish writers in favour of the validity of English ordination ; and, first, let us bear

in mind "that there is no *decree* of the Church of
Rome that declares the English ordinations null;"
next, that the practice of the Church of Rome has
varied in this respect.

In the year 1664 we find Peter Walsh, a Fran-
ciscan, writing as follows :—"I would certainly
hold myself obliged in conscience to concur with
them who doubt not the ordination of bishops,
priests, and deacons in the (Protestant) Church of
England to be valid. And yet I have read all whatever hath been to the contrary objected by the
Roman Catholic writers, whether against the matter
or form, or want of power in the first consecrators,
by reason of their schism and heresy, or of their
being deposed formerly from their sees, &c. But I
have withal observed nothing of truth alleged by
the objectors," &c.

Father Davenport (called Santa Clara) passes the
same judgment upon those ordinations as Walsh ;
for in his exposition on the 36th Article, he proves
from Vasquez, Conink, Arcudius, and Innocent IV.,
that our Church hath all the essentials of ordination required in Scripture.

Another fact, still better known, mentioned by
Father Le Quien, is, that a clergyman of the name
of Goffe, leaving the Church of England for that of
Rome, was admitted into the Oratory, (in Paris,) and
there was a talk of making him a priest; but he
having been already ordained in England, a difficulty arose. The matter was accordingly laid before

the doctors of the Sorbonne, who, having examined the question, " gave in the opinion that our orders were good." But the affair appearing too important to be left to the decision of a few divines, Rome was consulted, which enjoined the ordination, on the ground of the doubt still remaining of the validity of the English orders. Yet, continues Dr Prideaux, " the Sorbonists still stuck to their opinion, that he was a good priest by his first ordination." The Dean goes on to say that he had this from a celebrated (Roman) Catholic, Obadiah Walker, (Master of University College, Oxford, who joined the Roman communion in the reign of James II.,) who was at Paris at the time the affair took place.

In 1684, Cardinal Casanata having doubts as to the correctness of the practice of the Church of Rome about the re-ordination of the English, wrote to the Bishop of Castina to ask his opinion. This latter prelate, however, knew nothing about the question, and so at once decided that the English ordinations were invalid; but he afterwards, by consulting two learned friends upon the subject, was clearly shown that his judgment was wrong. It is also a well-known fact that Bossuet, Bishop of Meaux, did acknowledge the validity of the English ordinations, as appears by his letter to Father Mabillon in 1685; and this opinion he throughout life maintained, as M. de Riberolles, afterwards Abbot of S. Geneviève, who lived a long time with M. Bossuet, proves and certifies by a declaration, that he had often heard the bishop say, that " he had no difficulty about the ordinations made in the time of Edward and Elizabeth."

So, too, in the proposal for union between the English and Gallican Churches in Archbishop Wake's time, (quoted by Dr Pusey in his " Eirenicon,")—which proposal came from Du Pin and three other doctors of the Sorbonne—both Du Pin himself and the others agree in fully acknowledging the validity of our orders; and if one of them, the Abbé Girardin, is to be credited, the Bishops of Blois, of Troyes, and others, declared themselves in favour of their validity.

On this same matter, in answer to one who doubted the truth of the consecration of Parker, the great historian Dr Lingard says: "Though I despair of satisfying the incredulity of one who can doubt after he has examined the documents to which I have referred, yet I owe it to myself to prove to your readers the truth of my statement, and the utter futility of any objection which can be brought against it."

To all that I have now brought forward, no worthier conclusion can I add than the words of Archbishop Bramhall : " If there be any holy orders upon earth, the Church of England hath holy orders." And those of Dr Pusey : " There is absolutely no doubt that our succession is valid, that our bishops are the successors of those through whom God planted the gospel here; and so our Church is the appointed channel of God's gifts, and the instrument of salvation for us."

# THE SUPREMACY OF THE BISHOP OF ROME.

TO use the words of the present Bishop of Ely : " If once the supreme authority of the Roman Patriarch is conceded, all other Roman doctrines seem to follow as of course. And so it will probably be found that all converts to the Roman Church have been led to it from a conviction of the necessity of being in communion with the Supreme Pontiff, not from persuasion of the truth of particular dogmas." It is to the consideration of this claim to supremacy that I purpose now to devote myself; but before laying down the special points to which I would direct attention, the following words of Dr Newman, before we had unhappily to deplore his loss by his secession from the Anglican communion, may well claim a thoughtful consideration : " What there is not the shadow of a reason for saying that the Fathers held, what has not the faintest pretensions of being a Catholic truth is, that S. Peter and his successors were and are universal bishops; that they have the whole of Christendom for their own diocese in a manner in which other apostles and bishops had, and have it not." He now says: " Most true, if in order that a doctrine be considered Catholic, it must be formally stated by the Fathers from the very first; but, on the same understanding, the doctrine also of the apostolical succession in the Episcopal order has not the faintest pretensions of being a Catholic truth." "This," adds Mr Chambers, who quotes it as a preface to a sermon of his on this point, " may be tested by calling upon him to show that any ancient Father has called the Episcopate 'Antichristian, diabolic, and the invention of the first apostate.'" The grounds on which this claim rests are—

1st, That S. Peter, by our Lord's appointment, had a primacy, implying a sovereignty of authority over the whole Church of Christ.

2d, That he was Bishop of Rome.

3d, That this supremacy is inherited by his successors, those successors being the bishops of Rome.

The first assertion, as to the primacy of S. Peter over the rest of the apostles, has already been discussed in brief by the Rev. W. Denton, and incidentally by the Rev. J. C. Chambers; that it requires here but a passing notice, and leaves me at liberty to gather up the historical facts bearing upon statements 2 and 3.

In one sense we willingly grant to S. Peter a primacy over the rest of the apostles; a priority that is in quickness of apprehension, boldness of spirit, readiness of speech, zeal, resolution, and industry in his Master's service—he being, as S. Chrysostom

often says of him, "always hot and eager, always
prompt and vigorous." He had, too, a certain
priority of order, having been the first called; one
of the first, if not the first, that distinctly believed
our Lord's divinity; very probably, too, he was first
in age. But this priority of order in no way im-
plies a supremacy of power; for if there had been,
most certainly we should have found some commission of this kind in Scripture, but nothing of the
kind is to be found; he is called to the Apostleship
in common with the rest, but nowhere is he called
the Vicar of Christ, Sovereign Pontiff, or Arch-
Apostle. Indeed, there was no office known to
the Primitive Church higher than the Apostleship.
"This," saith S. Chrysostom, "was the greatest
authority, and the top of authorities;" S.
Paul's conduct alone sufficiently proves that he
owned no subjection to S. Peter, nor dependence on
him; nay, he hesitated not to "withstand him to
the face, because he was to be blamed." And this
argument from holy Scripture is sufficiently borne
out by the Fathers, for S. Cyprian says: "The
other apostles were what Peter was, endowed with
an equal share of honour and power." So also S.
Ambrose: "His (S. Peter's) was a precedence of
confession, not of honour." Similarly S. Jerome
and S. Isidore.

On the other hand, the argument in favour of
his primacy is based upon the well-known words,
"Thou art Peter, and upon this rock will I build

my church." Of these words many are the inter-
pretations, some, with S. Chrysostom, taking "on
this rock" as "on the faith of this confession,"
which S. Peter had just made of our Lord's divinity;
others, with S. Augustine, taking "on this rock"
to mean Christ Himself; and with these agree S.
Ambrose, S. Hilary, S. Cyril of Alexandria, &c.
&c., to say nothing of the important fact, hidden
in the original words themselves, viz., that our
Lord said, "Thou art Peter" (Petros), which word
properly signifies a stone or a portion of a rock;
but when He added, "Upon this rock I will build
My church," He used the feminine noun (petra),
which means an entire rock; so that if our Lord
had again referred to S. Peter, He would have used
the masculine dative (Petro).

Now, certainly others did understand S. Peter
himself to be the rock, as, for instance, Tertul-
lian, Origen, S. Cyprian; but this last-named
Father supposes that under this primacy of
one was typified the Unity of the Church; and
the learned Dr Barrow (of whose treatise I make
such free use) justly remarks: "Was S. Peter a rock
on which the Church was to be founded? Be it so.
But no less were they all: for the wall of Jerusalem,
which came down from heaven, had twelve founda-
tions, on which were inscribed the names of the
twelve Apostles of the Lamb; but the foundation-
stone was Christ."

Similarly, with respect to the next argument for

S. Peter's supremacy, derived from the words, "I will give unto thee the keys of the kingdom of heaven," &c., most certainly was it a mark of special honour to S. Peter that those words were first said to him; but only two chapters further on in the same Gospel (S. Matthew) we find the same privilege of binding and loosing given to them all. Still, both these are *promises*. But in S. John xx. 21, 23, this power is *actually conveyed* not to S. Peter by himself, but to all together.

But nothing that was said of S. Peter is so express for an universal supremacy as that which S. Paul said of himself, 2 Cor. xi. 28, that " *the care of all the Churches* " lay upon him; or, again, in 1 Cor. vii. 17, *So ordain I in all Churches.* So, too, when the strife arose among the Apostles, (S. Luke xxii. 24,) which of them should be accounted the greatest, might we not have supposed that, if a supremacy on the part of one of them had been so essential a point, and one upon which the unity of the Church should depend, our Blessed Lord would have graciously willed to return an answer to the question of the disciples. Nowhere in the Acts of the Apostles, or in the two Catholic Epistles of S. Peter, do we find any intimation of the assumption on his part of this supremacy over the rest; indeed, at the first council at Jerusalem, it was not S. Peter but S. James who presided, and spoke with the voice of authority, "therefore I judge." Neither is there any greater

force of argument contained in the injunction, "Feed
my sheep," for (I again quote Dr Barrow) it is not
said, "Thou alone feed my sheep;" nor yet when
S. Paul exhorted the bishops at Ephesus to feed the
Church of God may it be collected that each of
them was a universal governor of the whole Church.
Rather do the words to S. Peter, at most, only, as S.
Cyril saith, renew the former grant of apostleship.
Much more might be said upon this point; but I pass
on now to the more immediate object, the evidence
afforded by history.   The question before us,—Was
S. Peter ever Bishop of Rome?

Here it is necessary to understand what we mean
by the word bishop; for if we take it in the ordinary
sense of the word, then it is clear S. Peter, being an
apostle, could not become a bishop, for the two
offices are distinct in their nature—the apostleship
being an extraordinary office, charged with instruc-
tion and government of the whole world, but episcopacy is an ordinary standing charge, affixed to one
place, and requiring a special attendance there.  Now,
both from holy Scripture, especially S. Paul's writings, as well as from the ancient Fathers, we gather
that S. Peter was constantly going about to other
places, to Jerusalem, Antioch, Corinth, Pontus, and
Bithynia, seldom mentioned as being at Rome.
"Had he been Bishop of Rome," continues Dr
Barrow, "he must have given a very evil example
of non-residence:" and further, there was a distinct
rule that no bishop should desert one church and

transfer himself to another; and so strongly was this felt that the Synod of Alexandria speaks of Eusebius by passing from Berytus to Nicomedia as annulling his episcopacy; and this view is confirmed by synods again and again—nay, even one Pope, Damasus, ex-communicated all those who should commit this. Now, S. Peter is universally reported to have been Bishop of Antioch for seven years together; if, then, he passed from thence to Rome, all the Fathers and synods above alluded to must have forgotten that S. Peter had done the very same thing. It was, too, condemned by the Synod of Nice, by Popes Cornelius and Innocent I., that two bishops should preside together in one city; but if S. Peter was Bishop of Rome, this irregularity was committed, for the same authorities upon which S. Peter's episcopacy is built also make S. Paul bishop of the same. Against the assertion of S. Peter's episcopacy, which assertion never found any real support until the third century, we have the distinct statement of Irenæus, that "the Roman Church was founded and constituted by the two most glorious apostles, Peter and Paul, and that they delivered the episcopal office into the hands of Linus." Next, the apostolical Constitutions affirm that " Linus was first ordained bishop of the Roman church by S. Paul, but Clement, after the death of Linus, by S. Peter, in the second place. Other writers make Linus and Clement to have been Bishops of Rome at the same time—the latter of the circumcision, the former of the uncir-

cumcision, in accordance with the apostleship of S.
Peter and S. Paul. Others, again, mention Linus
first, Cletus or Anicletus second, and Clement
third; but all place Linus there during the apostle's
lifetime. To sum up, there is good evidence to
show that S. Peter was at Rome, that he assisted S.
Paul in founding the Church there, that in conjunc-
tion with S. Paul he ordained one or more of its
earliest bishops, and that there he suffered death for
the sake of Christ. But there is no reason to believe
that he was ever, in a proper or local sense, Bishop
of Rome, or indeed that in that sense any of the
apostles had a fixed episcopacy, (with the single
exception of S. James, who, for a special reason,
was appointed to preside over Jerusalem;) but that
he exercised at Rome, as did the other apostles
wherever they went, a supreme and hyper-episcopal
control, discipline, and government. In fact, the
whole argument makes out a far better claim to the
title of Bishop of Rome for S. Paul than S. Peter.

The third point is, that this supremacy of S. Peter
is inherited by his successors, these successors being
bishops of Rome. To this an obvious reflection
at once suggests itself, as indeed has already been
pointed out by Dr Barrow, and lately by the Bishop
of Ely, that if (as I have endeavoured to show)
S. Peter had no proper supremacy, and was not
Bishop of Rome, then from the first it follows that no
supremacy could be inherited, and from the second,
the Popes could not inherit from him.

But waiving the argument derived from this, I will now attempt to trace briefly the historical facts which culminated in the claim of the Popes to universal supremacy over the whole Catholic Church— all which tend to show beyond a doubt that this supremacy was a gradual assumption by the Popes, and also that it was in no way allowed by the Primitive Church; but, before doing so, there are two points worth noticing. First, That the Church of Rome, by her position as the seat of empire, and by the pre-eminence of her apostolic origin, was in very early times the object of a special respect and deference on the part of other churches; and this feeling was in every way a very natural one. Rome was, as it were, the centre of the civilised world; and as time went on there were few churches which did not owe some obligation to the Romish Church, if not as founding them, yet as strengthening and enlightening them; and thus it was that a primacy which might have been reasonable, became a supremacy which was pernicious: and so we are forced to this conclusion, that there was a tacit recognition of the claims of the Bishop of Rome to be first among bishops, *primus inter pares;* and that, however little we may be disposed to admit the validity of his claims to supremacy, it is quite certain that they never could have prevailed over the whole Christian world to the extent they did had not a primacy been allowed.

This first; but next it is well to bear in mind, as

the Bishop of Brechin, in his book on the Articles, remarks, that " by the code of the universal Church all jurisdiction in the provinces is given by the Metropolitan; but the Metropolitan himself receives his jurisdiction from the provincial bishops. The Pope, if universal bishop, must receive his jurisdiction from all the bishops of Christendom ; for, stripped of his patriarchal and universal powers, he is only an ordinary bishop. This militates against the Ultramontane theory, which maintains that the Pope is as much above a bishop as a bishop is above a presbyter. Such a position would imply a direct ordination from Jesus Christ, which, though a lógical consequence of the premises, has never yet been claimed."

It is also remarkable that the title " Mother of all Churches," which is the special title claimed by the Church of Rome, was given by the Fathers of the Second General Synod and the Eastern Bishops, not to the Church of Rome, but to the Church of Jerusalem. " Yet," adds Dr Barrow, " the bishops of Jerusalem, successors of S. James, did not thence claim I know not what kind of extensive jurisdiction ; yea, notwithstanding their succession, they did not so much as obtain a metropolitical authority in Palestine, which did belong to Cæsarea, and was by special provision reserved thereto in the Synod of Nice; whence S. Jerome affirms that the Bishop of Jerusalem was subject to the Bishop of Cæsarea."

Among the anti-Nicene Fathers nothing is to be

found that in any way supports the claim of the
Bishops of Rome to this universal supremacy, while
the Apostolical Canons particularly prescribe that
" the bishops of each nation should know him that
is first among them, and should esteem him the
head, and should do nothing considerable without
his advice." As also, that each one (of these head
bishops) should only meddle with those affairs which
concerned his own precinct, and the places under it.
Also, that no such primate should do anything without the opinion of all, that so there may be concord.—*Apost. Can.* 34.

There is still extant an epistle of S. Clement,
Bishop of Rome, to the Corinthians, in which not a
word occurs of any universal supremacy. In the
second century, S. Polycarp came to consult Anicletus, Bishop of Rome, as to the right day for the
observance of Easter; and here we find that Polycarp yielded in no way to the authority of the Roman
Bishop, for both determined to retain their own cus-
tom as to its observance, and there was no quarrel
between them, as Eusebius tells us, who adds, that
in the church, before parting, Anicletus yielded to
Polycarp, out of respect, the office of consecrating.

A little later on, we find the same question re-
vived, but by no means with the same good feeling, for the subject being a matter of discussion
between Polycrates, a successor of Polycarp, in the
see of Smyrna, and Victor, the Bishop of Rome, the
latter assumed to himself the power to excommuni-

cate Polycrates and the Churches of Asia, but
without avail; for not only does Polycrates affirm
that " he was not alarmed," but Victor's conduct
was at once condemned by the Eastern Churches,
and the Church of France; an epistle being written
to him in the name of the others by Irenæus, Bishop
of Lyons, warning him not to break the unity of
the Catholic Church.

In the third century, we have the famous
controversy about heretical baptism, between the
Roman Church and the African and Asiatic
Churches, when Stephen was Bishop of Rome,
and Cyprian of Carthage. The African bishops
unanimously approved of the practice of rebaptizing
heretics, but Stephen at Rome condemned it. This
naturally gave rise to bitter disputations, contro-
versies, invectives, and mutual recriminations; at
length Stephen, losing all temper, excommunicated
all those churches which agreed with Cyprian. He,
with the rest of the excommunicated bishops, maintained his own views, and strongly expressed their
disapproval of Stephen's attempt to make himself
" a bishop of bishops," and adds, that " every bishop
. . . . has the right of forming his own judgment,
and can no more be judged by another than he can
himself judge another" (Cyprian in Concil. Carthag.)
The same view is taken by S. Firmillian of Cæsarea,
who concludes an indignant protest with these words
respecting Stephen : " For while thou thinkest that

all may be excommunicated by thee, thou hast excommunicated thyself alone from all."

It seems, then, we have the fullest right to con-
clude that no evidence of the supremacy of the
Bishop of Rome is to be found in the first three
centuries; and this fact, were there no other evidence
to support it, would, to the minds of all who value
an argument based upon the teaching and practice
of the Primitive Church, prove conclusive. But
for those who doubt it there is no need to stop
here ; for the history of century after_ century
(history, let it be remembered, that cannot be denied
as a whole, being supported by writers of all shades
of opinion) proves the gradual increase of assumed
power on the part of the bishops who filled the see
of Rome.

The history of the fourth century is of the utmost
importance; for now we find the first mention of
patriarchates, and both the first and second Œcumenical Councils were held during this period.

It can easily be understood that Christianity
having been first preached in the chief cities of the
empire, the bishops of these cities, in process of
time, became possessed of certain metropolitan rights;
which up to this period had not received any de-
finite expression of opinion on the part of the Church;
but now in the sixth Canon of the Council of Nice,
A.D. 325, we find the following :—" Let the ancient
customs prevail, namely, those in Egypt, Libya, and

Pentapolis, that the Bishop of Alexandria have power over all these, since the same is customary for the Bishop of Rome. Likewise in Antioch and other provinces, let the privileges be secured to the churches."

It is clear from this Canon that the bishops therein mentioned are cited as metropolitans of higher rank than the ordinary ones; and the whole relation of metropolitans to the bishops of the province having been of political origin, it was designated at first by a name borrowed from the political administration of the empire, and so from the name of the civil magistrates presiding over the main divisions of the Roman empire, they were called exarchs, changed afterwards to the more ecclesiastical title of patriarchs. Of these there were originally but three, Rome, Alexandria, and Antioch,—all of them Apostolic Churches, which held this prominent rank; but soon was added that of Jerusalem, and by the third Canon of the Council of Constantinople, A.D. 381, it was enacted that " the Bishop of Constantinople should have the prerogative of honour next after the Bishop of Rome, for Constantinople is New Rome," by which a fifth patriarchate of equal honour was added to the former ones. The second Canon of the same Council has, too, an important bearing upon our subject; for it especially forbids bishops to go beyond their own dioceses to churches out of their bounds, or to bring confusion on the churches. It restrains the Bishop of Alexandria to Egypt, the Eastern bishops to the East, and so on ; it forbids any bishop to go out of his own diocese for ordination or in any other administrations, unless he be invited.

Not a word yet have we of any supremacy of the Bishop of Rome, but rather by implication the exact reverse ; for while on the one hand an equality of the five patriarchates is implied, on the other we have a decree of the Church of Carthage, enacted at a Council at Hipporegius (now Bona, in the district of Algiers,) A.D. 393, apparently with special reference to the authority of the Bishop of Rome as patriarch of the North African Church, which protested against the very title of patriarch, and would recognise the validity of no other title than that of Bishop of the first Church.

But this century does unfortunately contain the record of one Council—that held at Sardica, A.D. 347—in which certainly the first great step towards supremacy was given to the Pope. Hitherto, when bishops had been deposed, and had reason to complain, they appealed to the emperors to summon a larger synod to review their cause ; but at this time there happened to be an Arian emperor, and the orthodox bishops looked about for some other centre where appeals might be made ; and the Bishop of Rome (from the position which Rome herself occupied as head of the world, centre of civilisation, centre of orthodoxy) was by far the most important of all the patriarchs, and looked up to by the greatest number of bishops and clergy as their head. " Accordingly, in an unhappy moment, (continues the Bishop of Ely, from whom I quote this passage,) the Synod of Sardica, in its 3d canon, gave to Julius, Bishop of Rome, ' honouring the memory of S. Peter,' the power, if he think fit, to appoint the neighbouring bishops of a province to hear an appeal, 'and to send assessors,' such as the emperor used to send.  It added, by the 4th canon, that if a deposed bishop appeal to Rome, his place shall not be filled till the Bishop of Rome has heard the case; and by the 5th it decreed, that when an appeal has been made to the Bishop of Rome, he may appoint the provincial bishops to try the case, or send legates himself."  It must, however, be borne in mind that this Council was not œcumenical, but simply a provincial synod; and the wording of the canons shows that all this was new.  But the evil effects were soon to appear.  The case of Apiarius, quoted by Dr Pusey in his "Eirenicon," is an example.  An appeal had been made to the Bishop of Rome, (Pope Zozimus;) he rested his right to receive the appeal, not upon any inherent claim, but upon this Sardican canon, which, whether by mistake or intentionally, he quoted as a canon of the great Nicene Council.  Upon this the African bishops, and among them S. Augustine, declared their willingness to obey any Nicene canon, but stated they had no such canon as that alleged by the Bishop of Rome in their collection of Nicene canons,

which they received through him; and added, that
"they would comply with what had been alleged
respecting the appeals of bishops to the Bishop of
Rome, *until ascertaining* whether there was such a
canon of Nice." Accordingly they sent to the East,
and received copies of the canons from S. Cyril of
Alexandria and Atticus, Bishop of Constantinople.
In these copies, of course, no such canon was to be
found; and the stern address of S. Augustine to the
Pope informing him of it, at once sweeps away
any lingering hope that he might entertain of an
appeal to him (the Bishop of Rome) in matters
otherwise than of his own province. The fifth
century saw the assembling of the Council of
Ephesus, (A.D. 431,) the 8th canon of which forbids "any bishop to invade another province, which
has not from the beginning been under his own
authority," and likewise of the Council of Chal-
cedon, (A.D. 451,) which, presided over as it was by
the Bishop of Rome, was yet the means of the
heaviest blow that the Roman see had ever received; for its 28th canon, while acknowledging
that the Fathers of the Council of Constantinople
"properly gave the primacy to the throne of the
elder Rome, as being the imperial city," goes on to
say that the Fathers there assembled, "being moved
with the same intention, gave equal privileges to
the see of New Rome, (Constantinople,) judging,
with reason, that the city which was honoured with
the sovereignty and senate, and which enjoyed equal

privileges with the elder royal Rome, should also be
magnified like her in ecclesiastical matters, being the
second after her." Against this Rome had nothing
to bring forward, although Leo had artfully obtained
an edict from the Emperor Valentinian III., sanc-
tioning the primacy of the Bishop of Rome over the
Gallic and other churches; still it was of little avail
with the Universal Church. The history of the
sixth century is replete with the endless strifes of
the Bishops of Rome and Constantinople touching
this supremacy; but it is chiefly remarkable for the
assumption of the title of Œcumenical, or Universal
Bishop, (and which, too, was allowed him by the
Emperor Justinian,) by John, Bishop of Constantinople, which was violently opposed and denounced
by Gregory the Great, Pope of Rome, who, writing
upon the subject to the Bishop of Constantinople,
asks him, "What wilt thou say to Christ, the Head
of the Universal Church, in the trial of the last
judgment—thou who, by the appellation of Universal,
dost endeavour to subject all His members to thyself?" In a similar strain he continues, comparing
the unfortunate John to Satan himself, (*Greg.*,
Epist iv. 38.) In another epistle, too, he says, "I
confidently say, that whoever doth call himself
Universal Bishop, or desireth to be so called, doth
in his elation forerun Antichrist," (*Greg.*, Epist.
xxx.) Strong, however, as are these words, we find
in the next century, the seventh, that Boniface III.,
next Pope but one to Gregory, did call himself Uni-

versal Bishop, the words now used in the papal bulls, " We will and command," appearing for the first time ; and if his predecessor's words are to be considered infallible, must have been the Antichrist of whom Gregory wrote. But the limits of a brief Manual like the present forbid our entering into the full details which history presents ; I will, therefore, only note a few salient points as they present themselves in the following centuries.

But first let me quote from the valuable work of Mr Allies, " The Church of England cleared from the Charge of Schism," the following summary of the first six centuries :—" Had the supremacy of the Pope been the divinely-constituted government of the Church, the first six centuries would have borne witness to it. I assert that they have borne the most complete, manifold, and clearly-expressed witness against it. Nor can it be said that the same power was then visible in germ which afterwards so splendidly and marvellously developed into an august and consistent whole. The power of the Roman Pontiff in the fourth, fifth, and sixth centuries stood on a different basis from his power in the Middle Ages. The difference may perhaps be summed up by saying, that in the former he was Vicar of Peter ; in the latter, Vicar of Christ ; in the former he had a more or less defined Primacy ; he was first among brethren ; in the latter he laid claim to a complete supremacy ; he was exalted as a monarch above his councillors. A primate is one *idea;* a monarch is another. It seems to be the great *tour de force* of Roman writers to prove the second by the first. Rather is the true relation of the Roman Pontiff to his brother Bishops expressed in S. Augustine's beautiful words to Pope Boniface: ' To sit on our watch-towers and guard the flock belongs in common to all of us who have Episcopal functions, although the hill on which you stand is more conspicuous than the rest.' "

In the eighth century the Bishops of Rome began the practice of binding all the clergy, over whom they gained an ascendancy, by an oath of fidelity to the Romish see, while the power of the Popes was increased by the disposition of the highest dignities in the Church at their option ; while one Pope after another seemed to vie with his predecessor in haughty assumption. For instance, Pope Constantine I. suffered the Emperor Justinian II. to fall prostrate at his feet and kiss them. Gregory II. issued his anathemas on all sides. Gregory III. did the same, and dethroned Childeric, king of France. Stephen III. followed his suit ; and this Pope began his letters to Pepin of France, " I, Peter the Apostle."

The close of this (the eighth) century saw also that most remarkable fabrication (by a monk named Isidore Mercator) of " the forged Decretals," which purported to be the actual decrees of the Popes from the earliest ages of the Church, and of which Fleury the historian, who has given a full relation of them, says that " they passed for true for eight hundred years."

What Fleury draws out at length respecting them is stated in summary, not by English writers, but by divines or canonists in the Roman Communion—as Archbishop de Marca, Van Erpen, Constant, &c.— the language of all of whom, in reprobation of them, and of the incurable wound which they inflicted upon the discipline of the Church, is of the strongest possible nature.

Their object was of course to give unlimited powers to the Papacy, and with this endeavour, their statements—which, from ignorance of history and of criticism, were received as truth—were contradictions of the plainest and clearest facts in the history of the preceding centuries. It is, however, beyond my limits to enter into details; suffice it to say, the forgery was owned, " after eight hundred years," by all, even in the Church of Rome; and Dr Pusey, writing upon the subject of them, adds, " But the system built upon the forgery abides still. Our Communion was rejected because our forefathers used the same freedom which the Church of S. Augustine enjoyed."

The ninth, tenth, and eleventh centuries tell the same story, with the addition of the notorious characters of some of the Popes, culminating in the celebrated Hildebrand (Gregory VII.)

Of him it may truly be said, that whatever may have been his faults, it is " his commanding figure

which looms before us grandly as the overshadow-
ing genius of the Papacy during the eventful reigns
of six Popes, by whose sides he stands as the unfail-
ing counsellor and prompter, until at the culminating hour of time he chooses to seat himself upon
that episcopal chair, which, mainly through his own
fostering efforts, had meantime become actually
transformed into a throne of might" (*Cartwright's
Papal Conclaves.*) But no genius, however exalted,
can make true that which is inherently false; and
thus it is that the height to which Hildebrand, by
force of daring, carried the Papal prerogatives only
enables us to see more clearly how different was the
supremacy then claimed from the primacy respect-
fully permitted in the early ages of the Church.
Up to this time the title of Pope had not been restricted to the Bishops of Rome, but had been
equally shared by the Archbishops of Ravenna,
Milan, Canterbury, and other important sees; and
in the east by the patriarchs generally. The last
century had seen it somewhat restricted to the
Bishops of Rome, but under Gregory it was averred
to belong exclusively to the Roman Pontiff; and so
with regard to other acts of his predecessors, however far they had advanced, he went a step further.
Almost his first act after his accession was to claim
as tributary to the Roman Church the kingdoms of
Spain, Sardinia, Sicily, France, England, Poland,
Hungary, and others; and whereas his predecessors
had assumed the right to excommunicate and

absolve emperors, Gregory not only excommunicated
the Archbishop of Mentz, the Bishops of Utrecht
and Bambery, and the Lombard bishops, who had
deposed him, at the command of Henry IV. of
Germany, between whom and Gregory a great
quarrel had arisen, but he bound Henry by a like
anathema, to which the following extraordinary
sentence was superadded :—" I forbid to King
Henry, son of Henry the Emperor, who, through
an unexampled pride, has rebelled against thy Holy
Church," (he is apostrophising S. Peter,) " the government of the whole realm of Germany and Italy.
I absolve all Christians from the oaths which they
have taken, or may take to him ; and I decree that
no one shall obey him as king, for it is fitting that
he who has endeavoured to diminish the honour of
thy Church-should himself lose the honour which
he seems to have." "This," adds Mr Ffoulkes,
from whose history I quote this, " certainly cannot
be defended on the principles of the gospel, and it
is melancholy to reflect that it should have established a precedent." The celebrated Dictates,
which are ascribed to him, though perhaps not
written by him, yet embody his principles, as we
find them enunciated in his letters, and acted upon
by him. Of these the substance clearly shows how
the Papal supremacy was now regarded by those
who assumed it, for they declared " that the Roman
Pontiff can alone claim to be called universal, alone
depose and restore bishops, alone use the imperial

insignia, and alone have his feet kissed by all princes. That he can depose emperors, can be judged by none, and that his sentence can only be cancelled by his own act. That he can absolve subjects from their allegiance to the wicked. That no Council can be called general without his command, and that nobody can be reputed a Catholic who dissents from the Roman Church. That the Roman Church neither has erred nor ever will err" (*Ffoulkes' Eccl. History.*) His decree about investitures is a well-known fact in history; in fact, he seemed to carry all before him, the only person before whom his stout heart quailed being our own William the Conqueror.

The history of the twelfth century adds further examples of the pride and arrogance of the Papal See, of which I need only mention in proof the treatment which the Emperor Frederic Barbarossa met with from Pope Alexander III., upon the occasion of his submission to him after his excommunication. The emperor, we are told, after suffering much degradation, being at length admitted to the presence of the Pope, the latter placed his foot upon the neck of the prostrate Emperor, repeating the words of the Psalmist, "Thou shalt tread upon the lion and adder; the young lion and the dragon shalt thou trample under thy feet." These words he applied to himself and the poor helpless sovereign. It was this same Pope who made canonisation a privilege of the Roman See.

The thirteenth century especially commends itself to ourselves, as being the period during which Innocent III. occupied the Roman See, the manner in which he assumed to himself the power to dispose of the kingdom of England in the reign of King John being too well known to need repetition, together with his avarice, which showed itself in the public sales of indulgences, and the open venality of everything at Rome.

The fourteenth century bears with it the name of Boniface VIII., who, in his quarrel with Philip the Fair of France, asserted a power " to pluck up, destroy, and scatter abroad even kingdoms and empires ; that he could depose a king as easily as he could discard a servant." " Strange," says the Bishop of Brechin, " that the decline of the Papal See began with one who himself sustained its loftiest claims." For after exercising the Papal prerogatives to the utmost, " yet he died accused of every imaginable or unimaginable sin, (many charges *prima facie* being utterly incredible,) required by the French King to defend himself before a General Council.". . . The precedent of an appeal to a General Council against a Pope for supposed heresy or immorality was virtually admitted by the praise of Philip and the fact of the Council. On this followed what has been called the Babylonish captivity, the seventy years' residence of the Popes .at Avignon, subjects of the King of France, (Bishop of Brechin on the Articles, vol. ii, pp. 739-740.) The Bishop adds, speaking of the great Schism after the return from Avignon, "The shake to men's convictions by this event cannot be exaggerated. That the organ devised for the unity of the Church, as the Papacy, with more or less distinctness, had been recognised to be for centuries, in development of the teaching of S. Cyprian, should give way under the pressure and increasing strength of the adolescent nationalities of Europe, was a mighty blow to the Western Church." From that time history records the lessening and downfall of the Papal sway. Two Councils, Constance and Basle, claiming to be General Councils, and to have "their authority immediately from Christ," amongst other things, asserted the subjection of the Pope to a Council. Flatterers might strive as they would to keep up the semblance of the old authority, calling the Pope, as one of them did Julius II., "another God upon earth;" but it was impossible to restore again to the Papacy its former prestige.

But enough has probably been brought forward to prove the truth of the assertion which I laid down at the beginning, that this supremacy was in no way inherited from S. Peter, but was a gradual assumption by the Popes, contrary to the teaching and practice of the Primitive Church; and I am fully aware how much my argument would have been strengthened had I been able to enter into the great schism between the churches of the East and West, the determined opposition which the Greek Bishops ever offered to the supremacy of the Roman See,

and the repudiation of this authority in our own
land, and also into the intestine quarrels of the
Roman Bishops, in the case of rival Popes, &c. ;
but the Manual having already reached the limit
which I had proposed, its object being also a " brief
statement of facts," I am reluctantly compelled to
refuse, or at all events to postpone to a future time,
the advantage to be derived.  But there are a few
short extracts from a work lately published, from
which I have already quoted a passage (Papal Conclaves, by W. C. Cartwright), which are too important to be omitted; indeed the whole book reveals
a most extraordinary state of things in the election
of the Popes, which scarcely correspond to the notion
one would naturally form of a successor to S. Peter.
For instance, as a proof of the unlimited power
claimed by the Papacy, he says : "As an institution
regulated by palpable laws, the Papacy exists only
in the season of its creation.  The moment it has
been embodied it passes into the state of irresponsible
incarnation, above all conditions, all liens, and all
obligations."  In 1562 the gambling propensities of
the shopkeepers and merchants of Rome, which
came into full play upon each election of a fresh
Pope, had reached such a height that Pope Pius IV.
had to issue a bull, in which, amongst other things,
we find in the twenty-first clause, "Also, we forbid
wagers being made on a pending Papal election;"
the election itself being, as a rule, the scene of
disgraceful intrigue on the part of the various can-

didates and their friends; the pretences of the
cardinals of their being moved by the Holy Ghost
in their deliberations being a mere mockery, to say
nothing worse. "It must never be forgotten that
the election itself is a human act, and that human
impulses and weaknesses of all kinds come here into
play," writes Father Theiner, the present keeper of
the sacred records of the Vatican.

It is also worthy of note that there is nothing in
common law to render invalid the choice even of a
layman for the Papacy. John XIX. and Adrian V.
were certainly laymen; and the latter even died
without taking orders, and yet he promulgated
views modifying the whole system of Papal elec-
tions, which by his successors were held to be
invested with all the sacredness of pontifical utter
ances, (Papal Conclaves, p. 164.)

In Scudamore's letters to a seceder to Romanism,
the following remarkable statement is to be found
in the appendix. The writer is Archibald Bower,
the author of a history of the Popes, who had been
Professor in three Italian universities, and Counsellor
of the Inquisition at Macerata. It occurs in the
preface to his history. Speaking of the Papal supremacy, he says: "As I was then a most zealous
champion for the Pope's supremacy, which was
held as an article of faith by the body I belonged
to, my chief design was to ascertain that supremacy
by showing, century by century, that, from the
apostles' times to the present, it had ever been

acknowledged by the Catholic Church; but I was so far from finding anything that seemed in the least to countenance such a doctrine, that, on the contrary, it appeared evident beyond all dispute that during the first three centuries of the Church it had been utterly unknown to the Christian world."

In conclusion, let me honestly say that it is in no party spirit of hostility to Rome that I have gathered together these facts from history. In these days of trial through which our own branch of the Church Catholic is passing, one would far rather seek for points of concord than discord; but when statements are made which cannot be substantiated by an appeal to facts, it is at least the duty of every son who loves his Mother Church to take up arms in her defence. With this view I now put forth this Manual, that while I firmly believe our branch of the Church Catholic to be a true branch, our sacraments valid sacraments, our priests real priests, I yet earnestly pray that the Great Head of the Church, our Lord Jesus Christ, will in His own good time grant unto the whole Church that peace and unity which is agreeable to His holy will.

*Ballantyne and Company, Printers, Edinburgh.*

www.ingramcontent.com/pod-product-compliance
Lightning Source LLC
Chambersburg PA
CBHW021516090426
42739CB00007B/642